JOY IN THE JOURNEY

Recover with Color

CoDA Hidden Drawing Search

Find one of the hidden drawings in each of the coloring pages.

These are tiny, hidden signs for you to search for and color.
Enjoy!

Joy in the Journey: Recover With Color
is CoDA Service Conference endorsed literature.

Copyright © 2021

FIRST EDITION

All rights reserved

This publication may not be reproduced
or photocopied without written permission of
Co-Dependents Anonymous, Inc.

For more information about CoDA:

www.coda.org
info@coda.org
Co-Dependents Anonymous, Inc.
P.O. Box 33577
Phoenix, AZ 33577
Phone: 602-277-7991
Toll free: 888-444-2359
Spanish toll free: 888-444-2379

For additional copies of this publication and all
CoDA Service Conference endorsed literature:

CoRe Publications
www.corepublications.org
info@corepublications.org

ISBN: 978-9966052-4-3

Printed in Canada.

Welcome
of Co-Dependents Anonymous ©

We welcome you to Co-Dependents Anonymous, a program of recovery from codependence, where each of us may share our experience, strength, and hope in our efforts to find freedom where there has been bondage, and peace where there has been turmoil in our relationships with others and ourselves.

Most of us have been searching for ways to overcome the dilemmas of the conflicts in our relationships and our childhoods. Many of us were raised in families where addictions existed—some of us were not. In either case, we have found in each of our lives that codependence is a most deeply-rooted, compulsive behavior, and that it is born out of our sometimes moderately, sometimes extremely dysfunctional families and other systems.

We have each experienced in our own ways the painful trauma of the emptiness of our childhood and our relationships throughout our lives. We attempted to use others—our mates, our friends, and even our children—as our sole source of identity, value, and well-being, and as a way of trying to restore within us the emotional losses from our childhoods. Our histories may include other powerful addictions, which at times we have used to cope with our codependence.

We have all learned to survive life, but in CoDA, we are learning to live life. Through applying the Twelve Steps and principles found in CoDA to our daily life and relationships, both present and past, we can experience a new freedom from our self-defeating lifestyles. It is an individual growth process. Each of us is growing at our own pace and will continue to do so as we remain open to God's will for us on a daily basis. Our sharing is our way of identification and helps us to free the emotional bonds of our past and the compulsive control of our present.

No matter how traumatic your past or despairing your present may seem, there is hope for a new day in the program of Co-Dependents Anonymous. No longer do you need to rely on others as a power greater than yourself. May you instead find here a new strength within to be that which God intended—precious and free.

To a Loving Higher Power

To each member of the Fellowship of Co-Dependents Anonymous

To the codependent who still suffers

Acknowledgements

Joy in the Journey: Recover with Color is the result of a rewarding and loving group conscience process.

We would like to express our heartfelt gratitude to all who have committed time, energy, gifts, and talents to create this adult coloring book. We invite all who suffer from codependency to enjoy this book in the hope that many of us may find a sense of joy and freedom as we embrace our recovery work.

 # Calming Strategies

We came to CoDA because our lives were in turmoil and chaos, and we did not know where to turn. We were stressed, triggered, reactive, angry at ourselves and those around us. Walking into the meeting rooms of CoDA, we found a room full of loving, recovering individuals who were learning how to de-stress, deal with their triggers, respond to life, deal with their anger, and other issues.

This list is an example of the many options of calming strategies. We can use these strategies to help us de-stress, respond in love, deal with life, and learn how to sit with our feelings. In CoDA. we learn how to live in peace and serenity. We discover what strategies work best for us and choose to utilize them on a regular basis, learning how to live a joyous, happy, and free life.

- Connect with Higher Power
- Ask for help
- Meditate
- Take a walk
- Appreciate nature
- Make a gratitude list
- Call sponsor or recovery friend
- Read CoDA literature
- Journal
- Write a letter to HP
- Warm shower or bath
- Warm blanket
- Share experience, strength, and hope
- Make a God box
- Share
- Use pleasant fragrances
- Say a prayer
- Laugh, enjoy your sense of humor
- Offer service
- Exercise
- Read slogans
- Color
- Create art
- HALT - Don't get too hungry, angry, lonely, tired
- Visit coda.org
- Attend an extra meeting
- Use the telephone list
- Text someone
- Live in the present
- Daily affirmations
- Focus on breath
- Become mindful
- Practice Step Eleven
- Work Steps and Traditions
- Sing/play musical instrument
- Read *The Twelve Promises*
- Read *Preamble* and *Welcome*
- Be still
- Say the Serenity Prayer

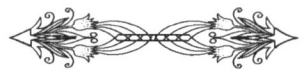 # Step One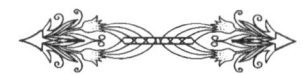

We admitted we were powerless over others—that our lives had become unmanageable.

POWERLESS

I learn to ask
"What do I want?" "What do I think?" "What do I feel?"[1]

I begin to see that I have not been given the right to control another person's behavior, but I have been given the responsibility to set limits and boundaries for myself with others.

"Step One is both the hope and the beginning of my spiritual solution. Working this Step allows me to identify, accept, and admit that I am powerless over others. What a relief!"[2]

 **A program of tools not rules.**

My Thoughts

Affirmation: I am enough, I have enough, I do enough.

Tradition One

Our common welfare should come first; personal recovery depends upon CoDA unity.

UNITY

I am willing to let go of my own ego and personal agenda in order to support the common welfare of CoDA. I learn to speak my truth and allow others the same privilege. By actively applying the principles of our program, I see that neither control nor compliance supports our common welfare and unity. I learn to listen, to have an open mind and heart.

In the Rooms of CoDA
*I learn to speak my truth.
I learn to care for myself
by identifying and expressing
my feelings, needs, and boundaries.*

💡 **You can't keep it unless you give it away.**

My Thoughts

Affirmation: I am accepting of others and myself.

Promise One

I know a new sense of belonging. The feelings of emptiness and loneliness will disappear.

BELONGING

"One of the program's greatest blessings is this journey we take together. We try to understand and support one another. We're able to renew our trust and faith in humanity; we see growth in people who work the program and look to the Fellowship of CoDA for support."[3] We journey together to live more fulfilling lives. We belong where there is understanding and acceptance, not judgment and advice.

Color me happy!

 The fruits of the CoDA Promises are delicious.

My Thoughts

Affirmation: I alone can do it, but I cannot do it alone.

Step Two

Came to believe that a power greater than ourselves could restore us to sanity.

BELIEVE

Doing what I have done up until now has not worked. These steps have worked for others for many years, so I am going to start to believe in a power greater than myself.

Today I can trust in a Higher Power that feels safe and right to me. My trust will grow. I can do this one tiny step at a time.

I can express my fears about trusting a Higher Power.

 **Steps are a road not a resting place.**

My Thoughts

Affirmation: I am willing to keep an open mind.

 # Tradition Two

For our group purpose there is but one ultimate authority—a loving Higher Power as expressed to our group conscience. Our leaders are but trusted servants; they do not govern.

HUMILITY

*We are all equal, we all have a voice, and our voice matters. No one governs.
The group conscience process offers us safety. We refrain from crosstalk, arguing, or shaming as we speak our truth. We remain open to others' opinions and let go of results.*

 **Say what you mean, mean what you say, but don't say it mean.**

My Thoughts

Affirmation: I trust my Higher Power's will is for the greater good.

Promise Two

I am no longer controlled by my fears. I overcome my fears and act with courage, integrity and dignity.

STRENGTH

I can trust myself because I am becoming strong, healthy, and whole. I have the courage to do things, even when I am afraid. I feel relief and I find strength knowing I am not alone. The time is now, today. I am changing.

The time is now, today.

My Thoughts

Affirmation: I am changing.

 # Step Three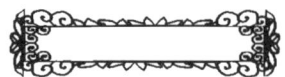

Made a decision to turn our will and our lives over to the care of God as we understood God.

EMPOWERED

The Third Step Waltz
Let Higher Power lead the dance.
Step One - I can't; Step Two - Higher Power can;
Step Three - I think I'll let Higher Power.
Let's dance!

A Step Three Prayer [4]
God, I give to You all that I am and all that I will be for Your healing and direction. Make new this day as I release all my worries and fears, knowing that You are by my side. Please help me to open myself to Your love, to allow Your love to heal my wounds, and to allow Your love to flow through me and from me to those around me. May Your will be done this day and always. Amen.

 **Higher Power is driving the bus. I can enjoy the ride.**

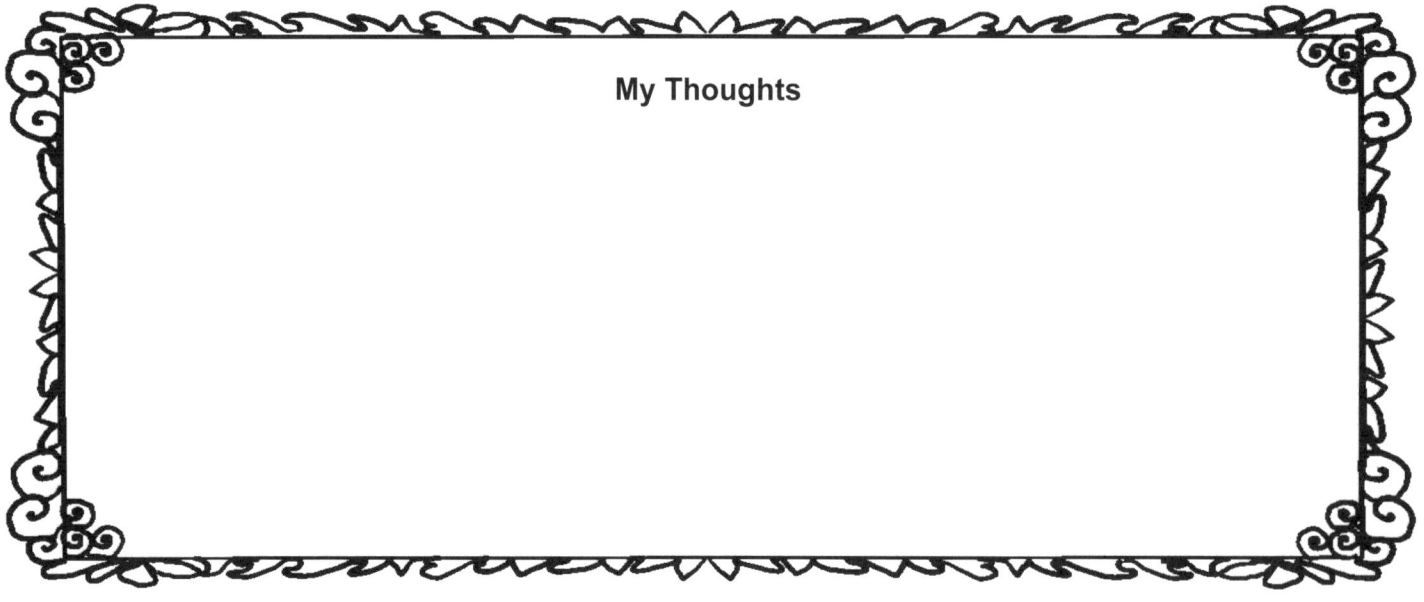

My Thoughts

Affirmation: I trust my Higher Power to give me all that I have and all that I need.

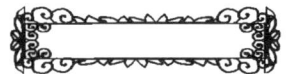 # Tradition Three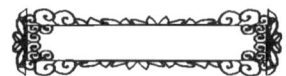

The only requirement for membership in CoDA is a desire for healthy and loving relationships.

WELCOME

When we love and honor ourselves, we have healthier relationships. In CoDA, we are learning a new way of life. All we are being asked to do is work our program, motivated by the desire for healthy and loving relationships with ourselves and others.

 Today, I will be the change!

My Thoughts

Affirmation: I am accepting of others and myself.

Promise Three

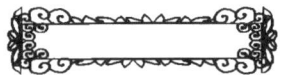 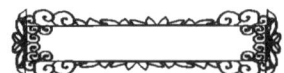

I know a new freedom.

SERENITY

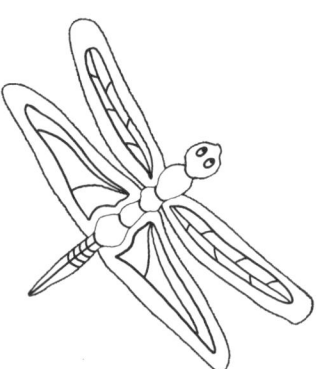

"My Higher Power wants me to let go of things that aren't mine. When I remember this, I feel lighter."[5]

I am no longer controlled by my fears. As I grow and heal, my feelings become clearer, and I reap the promises of recovery.

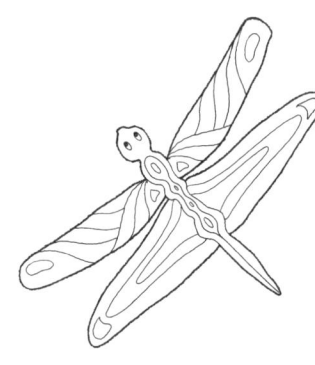

 **Freedom from bondage means freedom to live.**

My Thoughts

Affirmation: I am grateful for what I have and who I am.

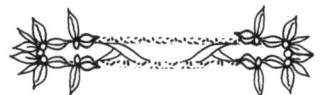 # Step Four

Made a searching and fearless moral inventory of ourselves.

REFLECTIONS

We are at the beginning of a spiritual journey, "on the brink of a great adventure, the discovery of our true selves." It can seem frightening but we also know that courage is not "the absence of fear but our willingness to walk through it."[6]

- What are some of my losses and pain?
- What are some of the lies that I believed about myself?
- What are my positive character traits?
- Where can I improve?
- Which people have experienced my positive side?
- Which people have experienced my codependent behavior?

 **The only way out is through.**

My Thoughts

Affirmation: I am healing on this wonderful journey, one day at a time.

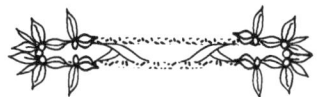 # Tradition Four

Each group should remain autonomous except in matters affecting other groups or CoDA as a whole.

WHOLENESS

"The spiritual principle of autonomy teaches us about healthy boundaries. Tradition Four shows us where we stop and someone else begins…that our decisions about our lives are ours to make. We may care what others think, but the final decision is ours, and nobody else's...Other parties...may be interested in the outcome of our decisions, but unless their lives are affected they aren't entitled to participate in the decision…when other people are actually affected by our decisions or actions, we become obligated to consider them in our decision-making…when someone else is making decisions about their own life, we don't have the right to control or dominate...In recovery, we may recognize that we have strong feelings about the choices our loved ones are making and we're encouraged to express those feelings."[7]

 **Trusting Higher Power is like taking the first step without seeing the entire staircase.**

My Thoughts

Affirmation: I give and receive with an equal partner, asking for help when needed and sharing my humanity with all.

Promise Four

I release myself from worry, guilt, and regret about my past and present.
I am aware enough not to repeat it.

 # RELEASE

💡 **Put down the magnifying glass and pick up the mirror.**

I feel worried about…   When I feel worried, I can…

I feel guilty about…   My calming thoughts on my guilt…

I hold regrets about…   My calming thoughts on my regrets…

Affirmation: I accept my journey as Higher Power's will.

Step Five

Admitted to God, to ourselves, and to another human being the exact nature of our wrongs.

ACCOUNTABLE

This Step takes trust in myself, my Higher Power, and another human being.

Being vulnerable is worth the risk, as we surrender our trust to those who are trustworthy.

The courage to share our truth brings us healing and spiritual light.

 **FEAR - Face Everything And Recover.**

My Thoughts

Affirmation: I can enjoy the journey.

Tradition Five

Each group has but one primary purpose—to carry its message to other codependents who still suffer.

HOPE

- The newcomer is very important to our program
- We share our struggles and our triumphs
- No matter how traumatic your past and present may seem, there is always hope for a new day

 **Yesterday is history, tomorrow is a mystery, today is a gift, which is why we call it the present.**

My Thoughts

Affirmation: I have a new hope in the program of Co-Dependents Anonymous.

 # Promise Five

I know a new love and acceptance of myself and others.
I feel genuinely lovable, loving, and loved.

CELEBRATE

- Today is a new day
- I love and accept myself as I am
- I practice gratitude and acceptance daily

 **Celebrate and be gentle with yourself!**

My Thoughts

Affirmation: Today, I choose to celebrate me!

Step Six

Were entirely ready to have God remove all these defects of character.

READY

"Step Six asks us to begin taking positive action toward changing those defects of character, part of our cleansing process."[8]

Am I sick and tired of doing the same thing?

Change takes time.

Can I be patient with myself?

I do not have to do this all at once.

 **Progress not perfection.**

What character defect am I ready to let go of?

Affirmation: I am ready to forgive myself and surrender.

Tradition Six

A CoDA group ought never endorse, finance, or lend the CoDA name to any related facility or outside enterprise, lest problems of money, property, and prestige divert us from our primary spiritual aim.

TARGET

*We are a Twelve Step Fellowship.
We use CoDA Conference endorsed literature.
We work a spiritual program.*

The goal is recovery, our aim is to listen to experience, strength, and hope. Spirituality is the key to our journey. Having a target makes the journey worthwhile and moves us to recovery. Outside influences are not part of this process.

 **My recovery takes practice.**

My Thoughts

Affirmation: I can learn to listen to others and keep my eyes on recovery.

Promise Six

I learn to see myself as equal to others. My new and renewed relationships are all with equal partners.

RENEW

Higher Power puts people into my life so I can learn valuable lessons in my recovery. I can appreciate and learn from others. In addition, knowing what is important to me helps me achieve my goals and enjoy life.

 **Expectations are premeditated resentments.**

My Thoughts

Affirmation: I am grateful for what I have and who I am.

Step Seven

Humbly asked God to remove our shortcomings.

REMOVE

This step is not results oriented; we ask and then let go. We become willing to believe our shortcomings will be removed by our Higher Power.

We trust our loving Higher Power. We accept that we have shortcomings, including fears, self-criticism, and perfectionism. We ask our Higher Power to remove our shortcomings. We become willing to believe they will be removed in Higher Power's timing. We then let go.

💡 **In Higher Power's time, not mine.**

My Thoughts

Affirmation: I am aware of my recovery progress.

 # Tradition Seven

Every CoDA group ought to be fully self-supporting, declining outside contributions.

SELF-SUPPORTING

"Self-supporting means that groups look within themselves for funding... [and to fill service roles.] Adherence to Tradition Seven protects CoDA groups from outside influence or obligations."[9]

I am self-supporting when:

- I do service work
- I share my experience, strength, and hope
- I support my meeting(s) and CoDA as a whole when I contribute 7th Tradition donations
- I have an equal say, and I participate in the group conscience process

"We may ask ourselves in what ways we contribute to CoDA in terms of money; time; attention; enthusiasm; energy; trust; respect; compassion; support; and sharing our experience, strength, and hope."[10]

💡 **Taking stock of myself is buying stock in my future.**

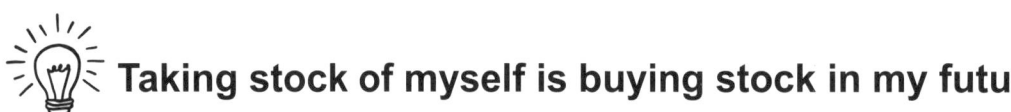

Other ways I can be self-supporting…

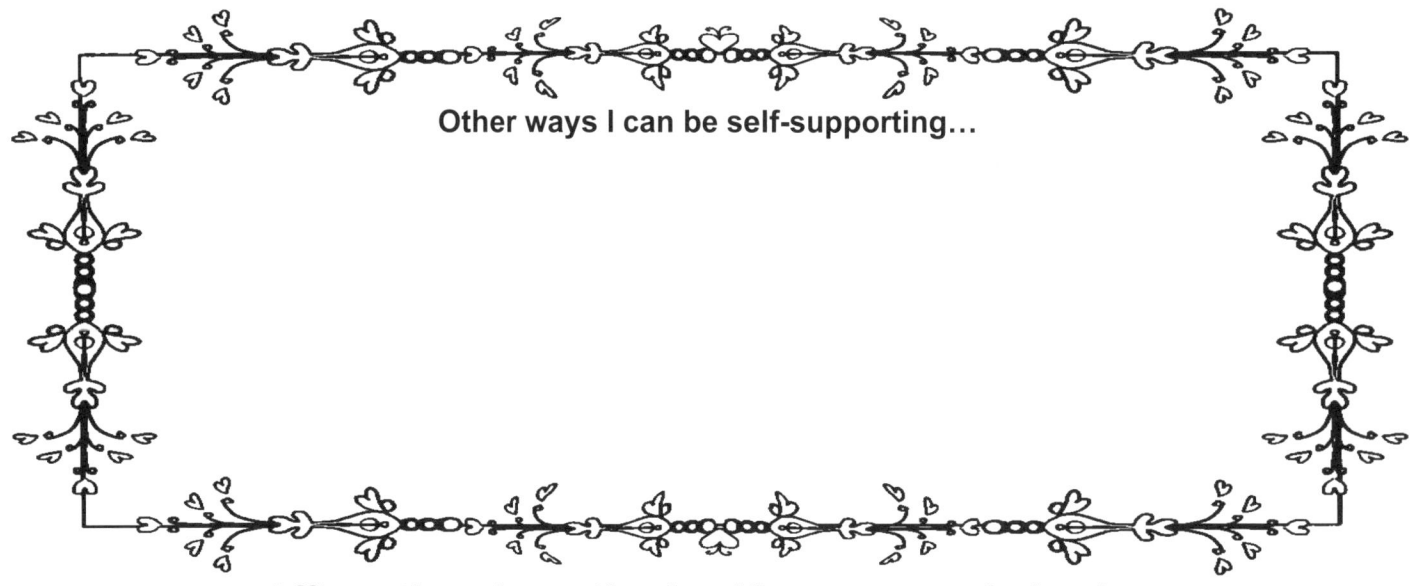

Affirmation: I practice healthy recovery behavior.

 # Promise Seven

I am capable of developing and maintaining healthy and loving relationships. The need to control and manipulate others will disappear as I learn to trust those who are trustworthy.

TRUSTING

"I blamed others when relationships failed. I was OK; they were selfish. I expected them to be perfect. If they had defects, I thought I could change them.

In CoDA, I've learned that I can only change myself. I accept that no one is perfect. Today, I love and accept others. I work on being honest in my relationships. Promise Seven is possible: 'I am capable of developing and maintaining healthy relationships'." [11]

 **Recovery is when I start living in the solution instead of the problem.**

My Thoughts

Affirmation: I have healthy and trusting relationships with others.

Step Eight

Made a list of all persons we had harmed, and became willing to make amends to them all.

WILLINGNESS

We made a list and began to be willing to make amends to our Higher Power, to ourselves, and another person for our behaviors and actions. Willingness is imperative to our recovery. Without willingness to be accountable, our spiritual program is incomplete, and we continue to play Higher Power, or give others that role. The HOW of our program is honesty, openness, and willingness.

 **Willingness without action is wishful thinking.**

My Thoughts

Affirmation: I am willing and accountable.

 # Tradition Eight

Co-Dependents Anonymous should remain forever nonprofessional, but our service centers may employ special workers.

SERVICE

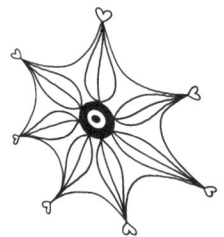

- CoDA meetings and service groups have no professional aspect
- This Tradition helps us maintain equality and humility
- Special workers may include accountants, lawyers, or administrative help
- Trusted servants are codependents in recovery, we do not look on them as professionals
- Being mindful of the servant position helps us remember our aim is a spiritual one, not a professional one
- This protects our program so our Fellowship members experience their own spiritual recovery

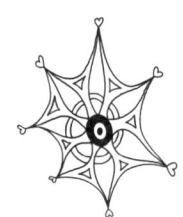

 **We are all equal in CoDA.**

My Thoughts

Affirmation: I know a new sense of belonging, and I grow through service.

Promise Eight

I learn that it is possible for me to mend—to become more loving, intimate and supportive. I have the choice of communicating with my family in a way which is safe for me and respectful of them.

RESPECT

- Our Higher Power creates good people
- Goodness dwells within us all, even those responsible for the broken promises and betrayals, abuses, hurts, and fears of our past
- It's possible to love these people yet not condone their behaviors; there is a difference between a person's "who" and a person's "do"
- We can love and forgive ourselves, just like we love and forgive others
- We are all learning how to value ourselves and value others

💡 **Love can't be bought; it is freely given.**

My Thoughts

Affirmation: I enjoy and appreciate the people in my life, including me.

 # Step Nine

Made direct amends to such people wherever possible, except when to do so would injure them or others.

ACTION

- Making amends is freeing
- Feel the fear and move forward
- Be honest with yourself and others
- Include yourself in the amends process, you matter too
- Surrender, let go, and let Higher Power
- When safe to do so, amends are made in Higher Power's timing

 **We only fail when we quit trying.**

My Thoughts

Affirmation: I can acknowledge that I am not perfect, and change is possible.

Tradition Nine

CoDA, as such, ought never be organized; but we may create service boards or committees directly responsible to those they serve.

RESPONSIBLE

- Trusted servants do not govern
- Our guidance comes from the *Twelve Steps*, *Twelve Traditions*, *Twelve Service Concepts*, and our Higher Power
- Rotation of leadership is important for new ideas
- Trust the group conscience
- Service is a beneficial part of recovery

 **Service gives wings to my recovery.**

My Thoughts

Affirmation: I am giving back in service that which I have received.

 # Promise Nine

I acknowledge that I am a unique and precious creation.

PRECIOUS

- Everybody is unique and precious
- It is important to be authentic, to accept ourselves, and to accept our imperfections and our abilities
- Our real value is found in who we are, not what we have
- I learn from mistakes; perfect is artificial but imperfect is real

 **I am my own best friend.**

My Thoughts

Affirmation: I am dear, precious, and valuable.

 # Step Ten

Continued to take personal inventory and when we were wrong promptly admitted it.

ADMIT

A daily personal inventory keeps our side of the street clean. We face our humanness, and we begin to understand progress not perfection. We learn to accept when we are wrong in our choice of actions, and we apologize as soon as we can. Awareness and an apology support our relationships with others and our Higher Power.

"Step Ten teaches us to review our behavior regularly."[12]

 **Procrastination is like a thief of life.**

My Thoughts

Affirmation: I surrender the results to my Higher Power.

Tradition Ten

CoDA has no opinion on outside issues; hence the CoDA name ought never be drawn into public controversy.

BOUNDARY

Following this Tradition, our Fellowship avoids public controversy. "CoDA has no opinions on anything outside of our Fellowship. Just as we avoid controversy on a personal level by not giving advice to others, we avoid controversy for the Fellowship by not offering opinions on matters unrelated to CoDA."[13]

"Tradition Ten also protects the spiritual nature of our program. We gather together to share our personal experience, strength, and hope of recovery from codependency. CoDA meetings are not the place to discuss our opinions about worldly topics. Honoring this Tradition, we provide a place of safety for everyone, regardless of religious or political preference." We remember, *"It does not matter who we are or what we do. It does matter that we work the Steps, follow the Traditions, and desire healthy and loving relationships."*[14]

💡 **Live and let live.**

My Thoughts

Affirmation: I listen without giving advice.

Promise Ten

I no longer need to rely solely on others to provide my sense of worth.

WORTH

"In CoDA, we learn that our self-worth and well-being come from our Higher Power. When we attempt to codependently control or manipulate others, we turn ourselves into a Higher Power to maintain our sense of safety and well-being. When we codependently avoid others, as well as adapt or change our behavior for others, we give them, instead of our Higher Power, this control and strength.

As we turn ourselves into a Higher Power or give the power to others, we leave little room for our Higher Power to work in our lives. This is our spiritual dilemma."[15]

 We do have choices.

My Thoughts

Affirmation: I trust my Higher Power's validation.

Step Eleven

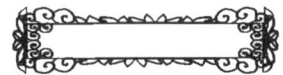 

Sought through prayer and meditation to improve our conscious contact with God as we understood God, praying only for knowledge of God's will for us and the power to carry that out.

POWER

"It does not matter how we pray and meditate; what matters is that we do it."[16]

"Daily prayer and meditation connect us with the God of our understanding and how we want to live today… We improve our conscious contact and increase awareness of our own reality, through prayer and meditation. We find the power we need to carry out God's will as we work this Step."[17]

Happiness is wanting what I have, not having what I want.

How do I seek God's will?

My way of prayer is…   My time of prayer is…

My place of prayer is…   My form of meditation is…

Affirmation: I trust my Higher Power's will is for my greater good.

Tradition Eleven

Our public relations policy is based on attraction rather than promotion; we need always maintain personal anonymity at the level of press, radio, films, television, and all other public forms of communication.

ATTRACTION

"Attraction is a force that draws things or people together...Simply by living our program, attraction is possible. When others recognize our changes, our serenity, our honesty, we begin to hear questions such as, 'How did you change?' or 'What did you do?'."[18]

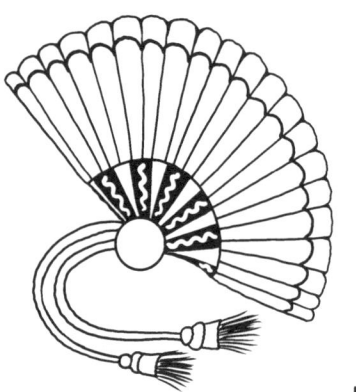

Tradition Eleven asks us to avoid promotion. We respect the choices people make to attend, to stay, or to leave the CoDA Fellowship.

Personal anonymity supports a boundary for each CoDA member to stay unidentified.

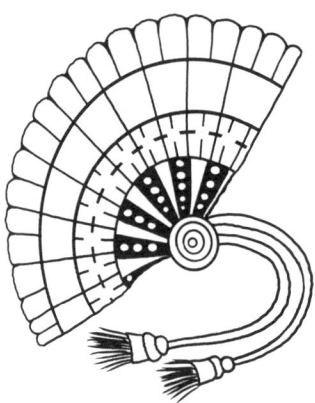

 A closed mouth gathers no feet.

My Thoughts

Affirmation: I am grateful for the gift of anonymity.

 # Promise Eleven

I trust the guidance I receive from my Higher Power and come to believe in my own capabilities.

OPENNESS

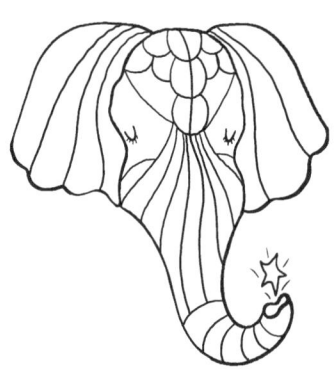

"I do not worry about the future or regret the past. The same power that causes the sun to rise each morning and provides light and sustenance to the earth can handle my issues, no matter how small or large. I am but one creation in this vast sea of creation, yet my part is vital...Although I may not always understand my purpose, I belong here simply because I am." [19]

CoDA Step Eleven Prayer

"In this moment, I quiet my thoughts and open my mind and heart to God's guidance for me. In this moment, I feel the gentle peace that conscious contact with God allows. If I am troubled and in doubt or joyful and serene, I turn to God. I know my path will be revealed and the way to my highest good will be made known." [20]

 **Success is the sum of small efforts.**

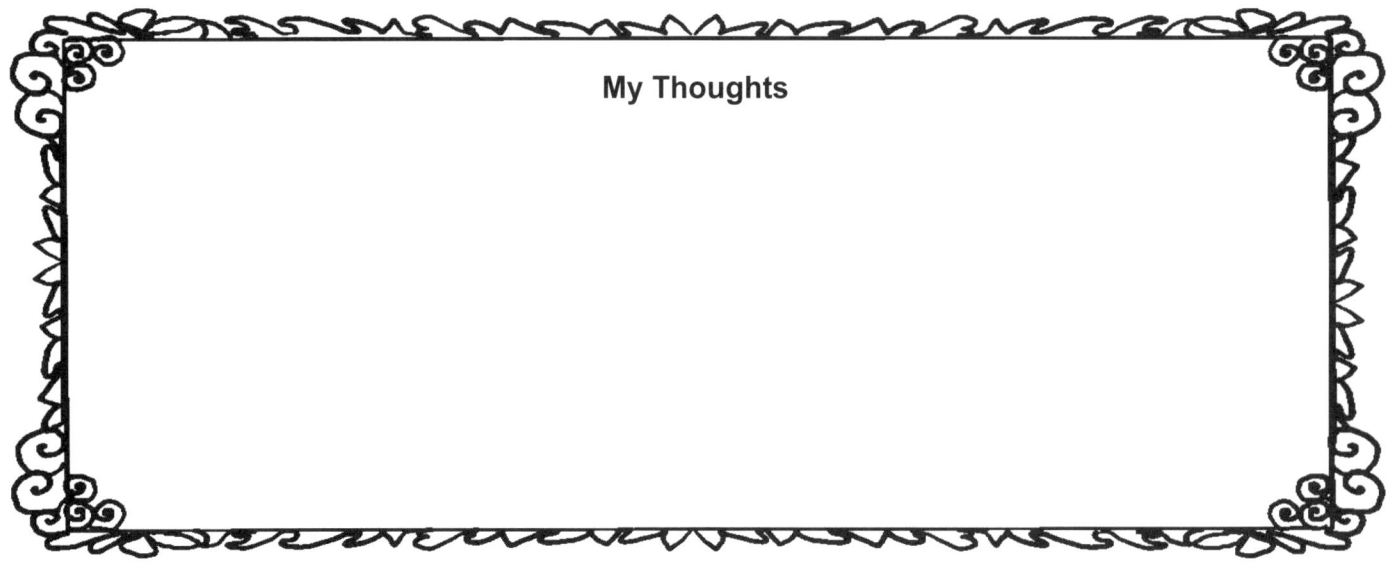

My Thoughts

Affirmation: With my Higher Power's help, my direction in life is clear.

Step Twelve

Having had a spiritual awakening as the result of these steps, we tried to carry this message to other codependents, and to practice these principles in all our affairs.

COMMITMENT

Our spiritual awakening involves many gifts.

- Transformation
- Hope
- Inspiring others
- Connection
- Higher Power
- Giving back
- Accountability
- Freedom

As we recover, we receive a connection to a Higher Power and members in the CoDA Fellowship. As we continue our recovery, we give back through service.

In what ways can I do service today?

 **Acceptance is important to my spirituality.**

My Thoughts

Affirmation: I have a sense of purpose in my life today.

Tradition Twelve

Anonymity is the spiritual foundation of all our Traditions, ever reminding us to place principles before personalities.

SAFETY

- I am able to speak without fear of being judged
- I am able to share my truth with humility
- I am able to embrace spirituality over personalities
- I am able to see how crucial anonymity is for my safety
- I am able to trust and be heard in a safe space

Principles before personalities.

My Thoughts

Affirmation: I accept myself as being who I am.

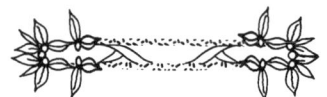 # Promise Twelve

I gradually experience serenity, strength, and spiritual growth in my daily life.

ACCEPTANCE

- I have a new patience with myself
- I have a new strength within
- I have a new awareness of myself
- I have a new tolerance of myself

 **Acceptance does not necessarily mean approval.**

My Thoughts

Affirmation: I accept where I am today.

The Twelve Promises of Co-Dependents Anonymous©

I can expect a miraculous change in my life by working the program of Co-Dependents Anonymous. As I make an honest effort to work the Twelve Steps and follow the Twelve Traditions…

1. I know a new sense of belonging. The feelings of emptiness and loneliness will disappear.
2. I am no longer controlled by my fears. I overcome my fears and act with courage, integrity and dignity.
3. I know a new freedom.
4. I release myself from worry, guilt and regret about my past and present. I am aware enough not to repeat it.
5. I know a new love and acceptance of myself and others. I feel genuinely lovable, loving and loved.
6. I learn to see myself as equal to others. My new and renewed relationships are all with equal partners.
7. I am capable of developing and maintaining healthy and loving relationships. The need to control and manipulate others will disappear as I learn to trust those who are trustworthy.
8. I learn that it is possible for me to mend—to become more loving, intimate and supportive. I have the choice of communicating with my family in a way which is safe for me and respectful of them.
9. I acknowledge that I am a unique and precious creation.
10. I no longer need to rely solely on others to provide my sense of worth.
11. I trust the guidance I receive from my Higher Power and come to believe in my own capabilities.
12. I gradually experience serenity, strength, and spiritual growth in my daily life.

CoDA Opening Prayer©
In the spirit of love and truth, we ask our Higher Power
to guide us as we share our experience, strength, and hope.
We open our hearts to the light of wisdom,
the warmth of love, and the joy of acceptance.

CoDA Closing Prayer©
We thank our Higher Power
for all that we have received from this meeting.
As we close, may we take with us
the wisdom, love, acceptance, and hope of recovery.

Serenity Prayer
God, grant me the serenity
to accept the things I cannot change,
courage to change the things I can,
and wisdom to know the difference.

My Thoughts

My Thoughts

My Thoughts

Preamble©
of Co-Dependents Anonymous

Co-Dependents Anonymous is a Fellowship of men and women whose common purpose is to develop healthy relationships. The only requirement for membership is a desire for healthy and loving relationships. We gather together to support and share with each other in a journey of self-discovery—learning to love the self. Living the program allows each of us to become increasingly honest with ourselves about our personal histories and our own codependent behaviors.

We rely upon the Twelve Steps and Twelve Traditions for knowledge and wisdom. These are the principles of our program and guides to developing honest and fulfilling relationships with ourselves and others. In CoDA, we each learn to build a bridge to a Higher Power of our own understanding, and we allow others the same privilege.

This renewal process is a gift of healing for us. By actively working the program of Co-Dependents Anonymous, we can each realize a new joy, acceptance, and serenity in our lives.

The Twelve Steps
of Co-Dependents Anonymous©*

1. We admitted we were powerless over others—that our lives had become unmanageable.
2. Came to believe that a power greater than ourselves could restore us to sanity.
3. Made a decision to turn our will and our lives over to the care of God as we understood God.
4. Made a searching and fearless moral inventory of ourselves.
5. Admitted to God, to ourselves, and to another human being the exact nature of our wrongs.
6. Were entirely ready to have God remove all these defects of character.
7. Humbly asked God to remove our shortcomings.
8. Made a list of all persons we had harmed, and became willing to make amends to them all.
9. Made direct amends to such people wherever possible, except when to do so would injure them or others.
10. Continued to take personal inventory and when we were wrong promptly admitted it.
11. Sought through prayer and meditation to improve our conscious contact with God as we understood God, praying only for knowledge of God's will for us and the power to carry that out.
12. Having had a spiritual awakening as the result of these steps, we tried to carry this message to other codependents, and to practice these principles in all our affairs.

The Twelve Steps are adapted and printed with permission of Alcoholics Anonymous World Service.

The Twelve Traditions of Co-Dependents Anonymous©*

1. Our common welfare should come first; personal recovery depends upon CoDA unity.

2. For our group purpose there is but one ultimate authority—a loving Higher Power as expressed to our group conscience. Our leaders are but trusted servants; they do not govern.

3. The only requirement for membership in CoDA is a desire for healthy and loving relationships.

4. Each group should remain autonomous except in matters affecting others groups or CoDA as a whole.

5. Each group has but one primary purpose—to carry its message to other codependents who still suffer.

6. A CoDA group ought never endorse, finance, or lend the CoDA name to any related facility or outside enterprise, lest problems of money, property and prestige divert us from our primary spiritual aim.

7. Every CoDA group ought to be fully self-supporting, declining outside contributions.

8. Co-Dependents Anonymous should remain forever nonprofessional, but our service centers may employ special workers.

9. CoDA, as such, ought never be organized; but we may create service boards or committees directly responsible to those they serve.

10. CoDA has no opinion on outside issues; hence the CoDA name ought never be drawn into public controversy.

11. Our public relations policy is based on attraction rather than promotion; we need always maintain personal anonymity at the level of press, radio, films, television, and all other public forms of communication.

12. Anonymity is the spiritual foundation of all our Traditions, ever reminding us to place principles before personalities.

The Twelve Traditions are adapted and printed with permission of Alcoholics Anonymous World Service.

References

All information referenced in *Joy in the Journey: Recover with Color* has been taken from CoDA Service Conference endorsed literature. This literature can be purchased on the CoRe website.

www.corepublications.org | info@corepublications.org

1. Co-Dependents Anonymous, Inc. *The Twelve Steps & Twelve Traditions Workbook.* CoDA Resource Publishing, Inc., 2018, p. 9.
2. Ibid. *In This Moment Daily Meditation Book.* CoDA Resource Publishing, Inc., 2006-2011, p. 65.
3. Ibid. *Co-Dependents Anonymous.* CoDA Resource Publishing, Inc., 2018, pp. 9-10.
4. Ibid. *Co-Dependents Anonymous.* CoDA Resource Publishing, Inc., 2018, p. 39.
5. Ibid. *In This Moment Daily Meditation Book.* CoDA Resource Publishing, Inc., 2006-2011, p. 234.
6. Ibid. *Co-Dependents Anonymous.* CoDA Resource Publishing, Inc., 2018, pp. 41-43.
7. Ibid. *The Twelve-Piece Relationship Toolkit.* CoDA Resource Publishing, Inc., 2018, p. 10.
8. Ibid. *Co-Dependents Anonymous.* CoDA Resource Publishing, Inc., 2018, p. 53.
9. Ibid. *The Twelve Steps & Twelve Traditions Workbook.* CoDA Resource Publishing, Inc., 2018, p. 101.
10. Ibid. *The Twelve Steps & Twelve Traditions Workbook.* CoDA Resource Publishing, Inc., 2018, p. 102.
11. Ibid. *In This Moment Daily Meditation Book.* CoDA Resource Publishing, Inc., 2016, p. 27.
12. Ibid. *The Twelve Steps & Twelve Traditions Workbook.* CoDA Resource Publishing, Inc., 2018, p. 134.
13. Ibid. *The Twelve Steps & Twelve Traditions Workbook.* CoDA Resource Publishing, Inc., 2018, p. 139.
14. Ibid. *The Twelve Steps & Twelve Traditions Workbook.* CoDA Resource Publishing, Inc., 2018, p. 139.
15. Ibid. *Co-Dependents Anonymous.* CoDA Resource Publishing, Inc., 2018, pp. 15-16.
16. Ibid. *The Twelve Steps & Twelve Traditions Workbook.* CoDA Resource Publishing, Inc., 2018, p. 145.
17. Ibid. *The Twelve Steps & Twelve Traditions Workbook.* CoDA Resource Publishing, Inc., 2018, p. 145.
18. Ibid. *The Twelve Steps & Twelve Traditions Workbook.* CoDA Resource Publishing, Inc., 2018, p. 151.
19. Ibid. *In This Moment Daily Meditation Book.* CoDA Resource Publishing, Inc., 2006-2011, p. 223.
20. Ibid. *Twelve Steps Handbookk.* CoDA Resource Publishing, Inc., 2018, p. 39.